AF228605

GIRLS' SOFTBALL

By Brendan Flynn

SportsZone

An Imprint of Abdo Publishing
abdobooks.com

abdobooks.com

Published by Abdo Publishing, a division of ABDO, PO Box 398166, Minneapolis, Minnesota 55439. Copyright © 2022 by Abdo Consulting Group, Inc. International copyrights reserved in all countries. No part of this book may be reproduced in any form without written permission from the publisher. SportsZone™ is a trademark and logo of Abdo Publishing.

Printed in China.
102021
012022

Cover Photo: Michael Turner/Alamy
Interior Photos: Jacob Snow/Icon Sportswire/AP Images, 4–5, 11, 31; Alonzo Adams/AP Images, 7; Matt Slocum/AP Images, 9; Kazuhiro Fujihara/AFP/Getty Images, 12–13; Sue Ogrocki/AP Images, 15, 27, 34; Kishimoto/DPPI/Icon Sportswire, 17; J. P. Wilson/Icon SMI/Icon Sport Media/Icon Sportswire/Getty Images, 19; Yuichi Masuda/Getty Images Sport/Getty Images, 20–21, 23, 36–37, 41; Takashi Aoyama/Getty Images Sport/Getty Images, 25; Shane Bevel/NCAA Photos/Getty Images, 28–29; Kyusung Gong/AP Images, 33; Koji Watanabe/Getty Images Sport/ Getty Images, 39; Michelle Lepianka Carter/Tuscaloosa News/AP Images, 43; Red Line Editorial, 44

Editor: Charlie Beattie
Series Designer: Jake Nordby

Library of Congress Control Number: 2021941600

Publisher's Cataloging-in-Publication Data

Names: Flynn, Brendan, author.
Title: Girls' Softball / by Brendan Flynn
Description: Minneapolis, Minnesota : Abdo Publishing, 2022 | Series: Girls' SportsZone | Includes online resources and index.
Identifiers: ISBN 9781532196379 (lib. bdg.) | ISBN 9781098218188 (ebook)
Subjects: LCSH: Softball--Juvenile literature. | Sports for girls--Juvenile literature. | Softball for women--Juvenile literature. | Team sports--Juvenile literature.
Classification: DDC 796.357--dc23

TABLE OF
CONTENTS

PITCHING WITH RACHEL GARCIA

The scoreless game entered the 10th inning, but University of California at Los Angeles (UCLA) pitcher Rachel Garcia showed no signs of tiring. The second-seeded Bruins were facing their rivals from the University of Washington in the semifinals of the 2019 Women's College World Series (WCWS). So far Garcia had quieted Washington's talented hitters. They had averaged more than five runs per game during the season, but Garcia had shut them out for nine innings. However, UCLA had also failed to score.

Garcia was focused on getting three more outs. Washington's leadoff batter in the 10th worked the count to 2–2. Then Garcia threw a fastball on the outside corner of the plate. The batter rolled a grounder to second baseman Kinsley Washington for an easy out.

The second batter swung at the first pitch and hit a foul pop fly near the Bruins' dugout. UCLA's third baseman Brianna Tautalafua raced toward the ball. She reached over the dugout railing and made the catch—two outs.

Garcia started the next batter, Emma Helm, with two changeups. Both were called strikes. The next pitch was her 179th of the game. Garcia fired a rising fastball that started at the batter's waist and ended up at her eyes. Helm swung and missed. Garcia had ended the inning on her 16th strikeout of the game.

The Bruins finally broke the shutout in the bottom of the 10th. An outstanding hitter, Garcia ended the game herself with a three-run homer. UCLA advanced to the finals, where they beat the University of Oklahoma for the WCWS title in a two-game sweep.

There were some tense moments in the finals against the Sooners. In the second game, Garcia gave up a game-

Superstar Pitcher

Garcia struck out 286 batters in 202 innings for UCLA during the team's 2019 championship season.

tying two-run homer to Oklahoma's Shay Knighten in the top half of the seventh inning. UCLA bounced back to win it in the bottom half of the inning. Garcia said her experience taught her how to overcome that stumble. "You've just got to flush it and move on to the next pitch," she said. "Because that's what's most important, how you bounce back from something like that."

UCLA head coach Kelly Inouye-Perez pointed out that Garcia doesn't allow many runners to reach base. But when it does happen, Garcia shows what she's made of. "What you do get an opportunity to see is how she can bear down and get herself out of those situations," Inouye-Perez said. "She's experienced, she's obviously very talented, but you don't ever see her get too high or too low."

Garcia threw all but two innings for UCLA during the tournament. She was named the WCWS Most Outstanding Player. She also took home the national pitcher of the year award and her second straight USA Softball Collegiate Player of the Year Award.

Cat's Meow

Garcia led the Bruins back to the WCWS in 2021. She then joined Team USA for the Olympic Games in Tokyo that summer. As one of the younger players on that squad, she knew she would not play much behind veterans Cat Osterman and Monica Abbott. But the experience set Garcia up for the possibility of future opportunities with the national team.

Pitch Movement

As Garcia proved against Washington, a dominant

Cat Osterman celebrates an out while pitching for Team USA at the Olympic Games in Tokyo, Japan, in 2021.

pitcher can defeat a team full of great hitters. Different pitchers approach batters in different ways. Power pitchers can throw the ball past hitters for strikes. But even the hardest throwers need their pitches to move. Straight pitches are easier to hit, no matter how much speed is behind them.

Osterman, for example, has always believed in ball movement as the best way to get outs. "Speed is not everything," the three-time Olympic medalist said. "I'm on the slower end of the spectrum, but the fact that I move it and I have the good combination of enough speed but enough movement is what's gotten me to where I am."

Putting movement on the ball is all about the grip. The way a pitcher grips the ball determines the direction in which it spins. Then the speed of the spinning determines how much the ball moves. A player can spin the ball faster by snapping her wrist just before releasing the ball.

Movement in pitching is more important now than ever before. In 2009 the pitching circle in high school softball moved from 40 to 43 feet (12.2 to 13.1 m) from home plate. The longer distance makes power pitching more difficult. Hitters now have more time to react to the speed.

"Pitchers now are doing very well working their spins and keeping the ball in play and making the defense make some

QUICK TIP:
ACHIEVING PURE SPIN

Putting proper spin on the ball can help a pitcher develop great off-speed pitches. When Team USA star Cat Osterman was learning to pitch, she would put electrical tape around the ball, creating a perfect line around it. She then tried to throw so that the ball would spin in a way that she could see the line the whole time it was in the air. Seeing the line—without any wobbles— let her know she had pure spin on the ball. "The more pure your spin is, the more sharp your movement is," Osterman said.

plays," said Bobby Pacheco, former coach at St. Mary's High School in Phoenix, Arizona. "There aren't a lot of overpowering pitchers now, but what the 43 feet has done to the pitching schemes is pitchers are coming back with more spins, more technique, and being more effective."

SLAP HITTING WITH MICHELLE MOULTRIE

Team USA was running out of time. It trailed Japan 1–0 in the sixth inning of the 2019 International Cup of Softball gold-medal game and needed a rally.

Ali Aguilar led off with a walk. That brought up Michelle Moultrie. Team USA's speedy right fielder had a chance to make it a big inning. She knew just how to make it happen.

Standing in the left-handed batter's box, Moultrie rested the bat on her left shoulder. She stared at the pitcher standing on the mound. As the pitcher went into her windup, Moultrie stood with her feet shoulder width apart and raised the bat slightly.

Keeping both feet in the batter's box, Moultrie then stepped away from the plate with her right foot. Then she crossed her left foot over her right as she shuffled toward first base. With another step, she slapped the ball into the ground in between the pitcher's mound and third base. By the time the pitcher fielded the ball, Moultrie was flying down the first-base line. She beat the late throw for a base hit.

With two runners on, Team USA had a great opportunity. Aguilar soon scored on Delaney Spaulding's single. Then Haylie McCleney's sacrifice fly brought Moultrie home with the go-ahead run. When Monica Abbott retired the side in order the next inning, the Americans had clinched the tournament championship. Moultrie's slap hit made it all possible.

Moultrie is a well-rounded batter. She proved her power by hitting 10 home runs in 61 games as a senior at the University of Florida in 2012. She hits for a high average too. She set the school record at Florida as a junior by hitting .443. And once she gets on base, she is a threat to run. Moultrie set the Gators' single-season (31) and career (83) stolen base records.

Slapping to a Record

Kayla Braud was the University of Alabama's leadoff hitter and an extraordinary slapper. She helped the Crimson Tide win the 2012 national championship. Before getting to Alabama, Braud had a national-record 103-game hitting streak at Marist High School in Oregon. "In high school, I didn't hit away a lot," she said. "I mostly slapped and bunted." At Alabama, Braud became a great all-around hitter. During her senior year in 2013, she hit .471 with seven doubles, a triple, and a home run.

Tim Walton, her coach at Florida, said Moultrie represents everything he's looking for in a great hitter. "If you could ask me what I'm looking for, I'm looking for Michelle Moultrie, a left-handed hitter that can hit for power, drop a bunt down, slap a ball into a hole."

One weapon that makes her extra valuable is the slap hit. In competitions where the slap is allowed, it gives a left-handed batter a running start toward first base. That makes it more difficult to throw her out. Moultrie's great speed is a huge weapon when using the slap.

Rule Change

Slapping used to be much more common at the college and international levels. But a few tweaks to the rule book have made it harder to execute. In 2018 a college rule change made it illegal to make contact with the ball if any part of the batter's foot is touching the ground outside the batter's box. That eliminated the head start that slappers had taken advantage of for years. As a result, fewer players are using the slap hit at softball's highest levels. The rule does not exist in high school softball, where players still use the slap often.

Moultrie has always had a rare combination of skills. She was a three-time all-state pick at Mandarin High School in Jacksonville, Florida, before her stellar college career. As a Gator, Moultrie helped the team reach the WCWS three straight years. In two of those, they played for the national title. Then she went on to play for the US national team, including at the Olympic Games that took place in the summer of 2021 in Tokyo, Japan.

None of her success is surprising to Natalia Gonzalez, her high school coach in Jacksonville, who said, "What sets her apart is her ability to lay a bunt down, beat out a bunt with her legs, and then hit a ball over the right-center field fence, and do it with ease."

In addition to her ability to hit for average, Moultrie has always had plenty of power.

The Slap Hit

In softball, a player can get on base many ways. The most common is a base hit. There are a lot of ways to hit the ball. Some hitters excel at dropping the ball down for a bunt. Some hitters are great at hitting stinging line drives to outfield gaps. Others are best at driving the ball over the fence for a home run.

Finding success as a slap hitter is a unique skill. It takes a great deal of coordination to be a good slapper. The hitter must be able to swing the bat while shuffling through the batter's box. She must have a good read of the strike zone. The hitter also must connect with the ball just right.

"Slapping is something that's not overpowering," said Kayla Braud, a talented slapper who won the 2012 national championship at the University of Alabama. "You're not trying to kill it. You're trying to hit it to the right spot. The goal is to [have the bat swing] on a plane and hit the top of the ball and get a nice hop. You don't want to hit it hard, just nice and smooth. It's an art, really."

Slap hitters typically hit left-handed. That puts the batter closer to first base. Usually, slappers are fast players who are also good contact hitters.

QUICK TIP:
FOOTWORK

All great slap hitters know that correct footwork is key to a successful hit. Players can practice their footwork at home or on the field. Just make sure there is enough room to move. First, get into a standard batting stance. Then step back with the right foot. Next comes the crossover step. This provides the hitter with the explosion needed to hit the ball. Cross over with the left foot and swing the bat. Continue practicing that motion, and it will become more comfortable.

Caitlin Lowe chokes up on the bat for a slap swing while playing for Team USA.

Former Team USA star Caitlin Lowe is one of the greatest slap artists in softball history. She said the key to being successful is getting comfortable with the unique motion of slapping. "The hardest part about slapping is hitting in basically a pretzel position," she said. "So, if you can make yourself comfortable with that contact point, then you're going to be able to run through and do it easier."

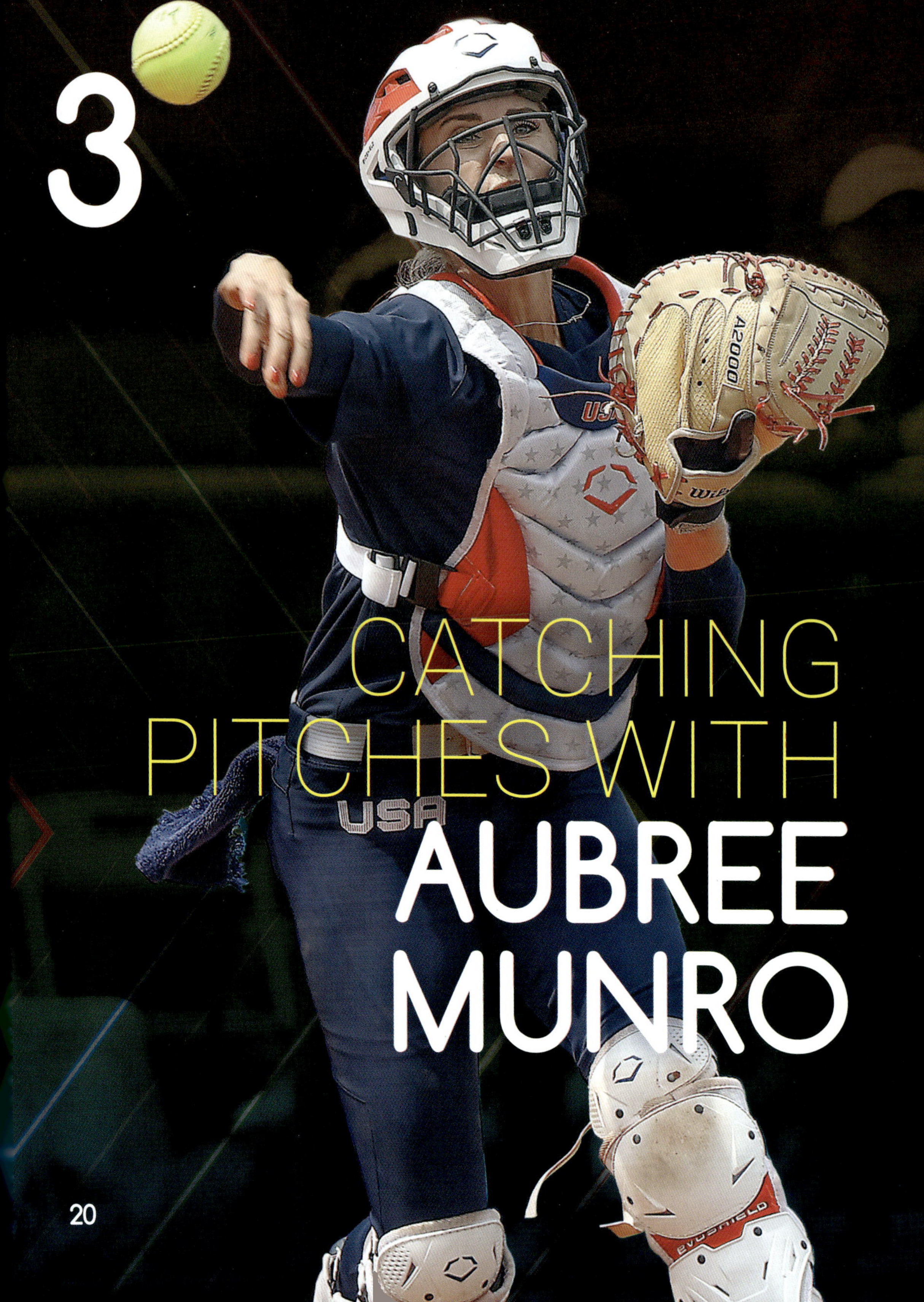

3
CATCHING PITCHES WITH AUBREE MUNRO

Standing behind home plate, Team USA catcher Aubree Munro assessed the situation. It was July 2021, and the United States was facing Australia at the Olympics in Tokyo. There were two outs in the eighth inning. Pitcher Monica Abbott had just given up a run on a bases-loaded walk, putting Australia on top 1−0. With the game now in extra innings, the pressure was on.

Team USA needed to limit the damage if it wanted a chance to come back in the bottom of the inning. Munro crouched behind the plate as Australia's Tarni Stepto dug into the batter's box. Abbott's first pitch was high and inside. Stepto swung through it for strike one.

The next pitch touched the outside corner of the strike zone. Munro squeezed it in her glove and turned her hand to the inside. "Strike!" yelled the umpire.

Abbott's third pitch crossed the inside corner of the plate. Munro caught it and subtly turned her glove inward. She held the pitch over the plate for an extra beat, making sure the umpire got a good look at it.

"Strike three!" yelled the umpire. The rally was over. Team USA then scored twice in the bottom of the inning to win the game. Abbott got credit for the key strikeout in the box score. But pitchers know what a difference a great catcher can make. A catcher who knows how to frame pitches plays a key role in getting strike calls on close pitches.

One Big Difference

Catchers in softball and baseball have many of the same responsibilities and challenges. But Munro said there is one major difference of how catchers frame pitches. "In softball we try to reach out in front a little more so the umpire can see over us," Munro said. "I know in baseball they like to catch it deeper and have softer hands, which is still really important, but because of the flight of their ball coming down, it's more difficult to catch it out front."

Munro has been doing that for years. She began playing catcher for her under-8 team in California. Her mother was the coach. The team had a hard-throwing pitcher. Munro's mom was having a tough time finding volunteers to catch her. But Munro loved the challenge. "The first ball hit me right in the stomach and everybody came rushing out. I was like, 'Oh my gosh, I didn't feel a thing. This is so cool!'" Munro said. "I felt like a Transformer. I've been catching ever since."

Munro, *right*, and pitcher Monica Abbott discuss strategy during the gold-medal game at the Tokyo Olympics.

Munro starred at the University of Florida, where she helped lead the Gators to two national titles. She began playing for Team USA and developed a reputation as an outstanding defensive catcher. Munro excels at pitch framing, blocking pitches in the dirt, and throwing out would-be base stealers.

Framing Pitches

A dominating pitcher can help a softball team win a lot of games. A good catcher who knows how to frame pitches can make a pitcher a little more dominant. "I think framing is particularly important because it makes your pitcher feel really good, and I think our job as catchers is to buy into whatever the pitcher needs from me, I'm going to do it," Munro said. "The freer a pitcher feels, probably the better they're going to throw."

Nuveman One of the Best

One of the best catchers the US national team has ever had was Stacey Nuveman. She helped Team USA win Olympic gold medals in 2000 and 2004 and a silver medal in 2008. Nuveman was a four-time All-American at UCLA as well. She was a powerful hitter who hit more home runs than anybody in college history. But Nuveman is probably best known for her catching. She was behind the plate for many of the Team USA greats, including Cat Osterman, Jennie Finch, and Monica Abbott.

Pitching strategy begins before the pitch is thrown. First the pitcher and catcher work together and decide what pitch to use. They decide whether the pitch should be fast or slow, inside or outside. Then the catcher sets up to the side of the plate where the pitch is supposed to go. Finally, the pitch is released.

Some pitches are clearly out of the strike zone. Some are right over the plate. Catchers can't do much with either of those. On pitches that are questionable, the umpire needs to make a quick call. That is where the catcher's job becomes more important. A slight movement of the catcher's wrist after she catches the ball can make a pitch just off the plate look more like a strike.

If she turns the glove the wrong way, a strike might look like a ball.

The better the pitch looks after it gets to the catcher, the more likely the umpire is to call it a strike. Those little movements can make all the difference. "[I try] to make my movements really quiet," Munro said of her framing technique. "I'm not trying to fool an umpire; I'm just trying to make a pitch look a little bit better."

Former Team USA catcher Ashley Holcombe said the first thing a catcher needs to learn is to be relaxed behind the plate. Limiting movement, especially arm movement, is crucial to good framing. The more movement an umpire sees, the less likely he or she is to call a strike. When Munro catches pitches, she does so with a straight arm and a stiff wrist. She catches the outside of the ball and turns it slightly toward the plate with her fingers.

Megan Willis was a great catcher for years. She worked with star pitcher Cat Osterman at the University of Texas and for the Florida Pride in the National Pro Fastpitch league. "When going out and receiving the pitch, number one, I want you to

QUICK TIP:
LEARNING TO FRAME

When practicing pitch framing, former Team USA catcher Ashley Holcombe said to focus on one side of the ball. For inside and outside pitches, she said, "I want to try to think about catching the outside of the ball." For a high pitch, Holcombe focuses on the top of the ball. "You don't want to catch it straight up because it's going to appear higher in the strike zone. And it's going to take your arm back and there's no chance the umpire is going to call it a strike."

think about catching the ball so the ball is facing home plate," Willis said.

In addition to turning the ball to the plate, Willis said body movement plays a key role in selling pitches. "Think about getting your nose and your shoulders behind the pitch," she said. "If that ball takes you a little bit farther to the inside or to the left, not only are you going to get your hand out there, but now you're going to shift your shoulders and nose behind it."

Framing is a skill that takes time to master. But it is worth it. When a catcher is good at selling pitches, a softball team can get a lot of strikeouts.

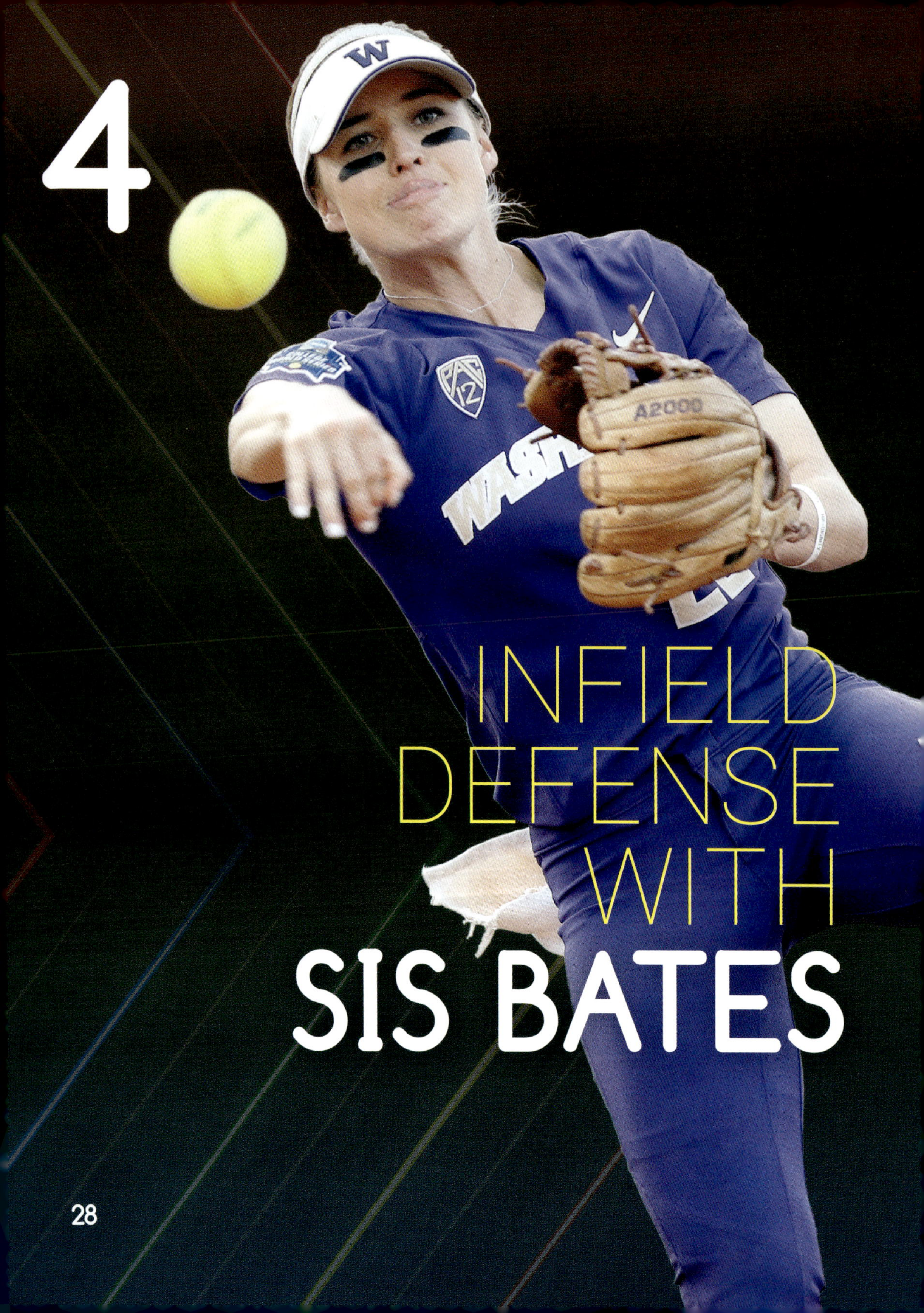

4

Nicole "Sis" Bates has a habit of making outstanding defensive plays. And her fans have made a habit of posting them online.

The internet is filled with defensive gems made by the former University of Washington shortstop. It's not hard to find videos of her charging ground balls and throwing off-balance to nail the runner at first base. In others, she fields grounders back near the outfield grass. She then uses her lightning-quick release and powerful arm to record outs.

In a game against the University of California, she set up deep in the hole to guard against a slap hit. But the ball bounced up the middle. It looked headed to the outfield. Bates took two quick steps to her left and stabbed the grounder. Then she used her momentum to complete a 360-degree spin and fired on target to first base for the out.

It was just another play for Bates, who won her third Pac-12 Conference Defensive Player

Sis Bates makes an off-balance throw from shortstop while playing for the University of Washington in 2018.

Bates with the Bat

Sis Bates is known for her defense, but she's no slouch at the plate. She left the University of Washington as the school's all-time leader with 320 hits and 18 triples. She was also remarkably consistent. In her last three full seasons, she posted batting averages of .389, .387, and .389. During the pandemic-shortened 2020 season, Bates hit an incredible .529 with 27 hits in just 15 games.

of the Year Award in 2021. "I would say 'unbelievable' but this is what Sis Bates does," one TV announcer said after Bates made another jaw-dropping play. "She's a walking highlight reel. She's the best shortstop in the nation."

While her flashy plays earned attention, Bates's steady defense was a key factor in the Huskies reaching the WCWS each year from 2017 to 2019. In 2021 she played every inning for Washington. She made just three errors in 59 games. She was consistent and reliable at one of the sport's most important positions. Her coach did not take that for granted. "She converts most of the balls she can get to into outs; that's as good as having a dominant pitcher," Washington head coach Heather Tarr said. "Whether it's routine or not a routine play. She's super efficient."

Bates's outstanding performance in 2021 earned her the national defensive player of the year award from *Softball America.* Only 12 graduating college players were selected to

Bates's flashy glove work led to frequent highlights during her college career.

participate in the Athletes Unlimited professional league that summer. Bates was one of them.

Bates earned her nickname as a kid. She would tag along with older brother Jimmy and play pickup sports with him and his friends. She developed more than her athletic skills. That's also where she honed her toughness and drive to win. "She's kind of a spitfire and fiery and competitive," Tarr said. "You don't like her when you're on the other team, because you know she helps [her team] win. So you love to hate her as a competitor. But you definitely want her in your tent."

Fielding Grounders

Perhaps the most important defensive skill to learn is fielding ground balls. An infielder who knows how to successfully field ground balls can prevent a lot of hits and runs.

The first step to being a good fielder is to have no fear. Sometimes, the ball comes very hard and fast at a fielder. She can't be afraid to get in front of it and use her body to make a stop.

The next step is being in the ready position. A fielder's feet must be square. Her eyes need to be on the ball. She must be ready to move in any direction. From the ready position, a good infielder needs to react quickly when the ball is hit. She has to be prepared for both a low ground ball or one that takes a high hop. That's why many of the best fielders have strong legs and good flexibility.

Huskies Tradition

When Bates arrived on campus to play for Washington, she had to change positions to make the starting lineup as a freshman. Senior Ali Aguilar was a four-year starting shortstop for the Huskies. So Bates played second base her first year. Aguilar, a three-time all-Pac-12 first-team selection, went on to play for Team USA. Aguilar started all six games at second base in the Tokyo Olympics in July 2021.

"Our goal with infielders is to make them look like the smoothest thing you've ever seen, like they're gliding on ice," said Patty Gasso, head coach of the University of Oklahoma Sooners, who won their fifth WCWS title in 2021. "We work a lot on quick steps and reactions. A lot of what we do is aimed at making sure our legs are strong enough so that we can move quickly from a ready position."

Bates lines up a throw while playing for the US national team in 2019.

Getting to the ball fast is only part of the job. A fielder must know how to handle the ball too. Fielders must be prepared to secure the ball with the glove and then transfer it to the throwing hand. Most infielders, including Bates, practice their technique over and over. That way they can make a smooth and natural motion from fielding the ball to throwing it.

After securing the ball, an infielder has one final difficult task—the throw. Sometimes, the fielder has time to set her feet and make a solid throw to the base. That's not always the case, however. Some plays require an off-balance or hurried throw. Because of that, it's important to practice all types of throwing situations. "We get them to throw at different angles to simulate the plays they're going to have to make during a game," Gasso said.

Practicing the fundamentals of fielding ground balls can make a good player even better. It certainly worked for Bates as she turned herself into one of the greatest defensive players in college softball history.

QUICK TIP:
REPETITION IS KEY

A simple way to give an infielder a lot of practice is to have another person roll ground balls to her. This allows the infielder to work on different types of ground balls and then complete the play with a throw. "The purpose for this is really to work on glove positioning, to work on footwork, and it really gives you a great opportunity to get a lot of repetition in a short amount of time," said Mike Candrea, who retired as head coach at the University of Arizona in 2021. Candrea coached Team USA to Olympic gold in 2004 and silver in 2008.

5

BASE RUNNING WITH HAYLIE MCCLENEY

aylie McCleney is an excellent hitter and an outstanding fielder. But she can truly change a game when she's running the bases.

McCleney played center field and batted leadoff for Team USA at the Tokyo Olympic Games in July 2021. She was a key part of the team's offense. McCleney played in all six games and scored four of Team USA's nine runs.

In the fifth inning of a scoreless game against Canada, McCleney blooped a single to short left field. She moved to second on a sacrifice bunt by Janie Reed. That put her in scoring position. McCleney bounced off the base, ready to sprint as soon as teammate Amanda Chidester made contact. When Chidester lined a single to right field, McCleney was off. She raced to third, made a sharp turn and sprinted home. That play scored the only run of Team USA's 1–0 win.

Haylie McCleney takes off for first base after hitting a single against Mexico at the Olympic Games in Tokyo.

Leading off the next game against Mexico, McCleney showed off her speed. She hit a ground ball up the middle.

Leading the Nation

University of Central Arkansas freshman Jenna Wildeman led all Division I players with 56 stolen bases in 2021. She was only thrown out three times all season. And twice she stole four bases in a game. "It was really something special, and I hope she can continue to do that," head coach David Kuhn said of Wildeman's remarkable season.

The second baseman made a nice play, but McCleney beat the throw to first. The next two hitters failed to move her around the bases. So she decided to take matters into her own hands—or feet. Just as Mexico's pitcher released the ball, McCleney broke for second. She timed the steal perfectly and was safe. The United States did not score in the inning, but two innings later McCleney singled again. This time she came around to score on Ali Aguilar's two-run single. That proved to be the winning run in a 2–0 victory.

Later in the tournament, the United States trailed Australia 1–0 in the bottom of the eighth inning. Team USA had to score to keep the game going. With Aubree Munro on second and nobody out, McCleney hit a routine grounder to shortstop. The fielder hesitated ever so slightly. McCleney beat the throw to first after getting a great jump out of the batter's box.

McCleney has been a regular for the US national team since 2016 and won a silver medal at the Olympics in 2021.

Reed sacrificed to move the runners up a base. Once again, Chidester delivered a key base hit. Munro scored easily. McCleney hustled around third with an efficient turn. Australia's left fielder had no chance to throw her out. She crossed the plate to give Team USA a dramatic 2–1 victory.

Excellent base running can be the difference between winning and losing a game. But a player can't show off good base running if she can't reach base. McCleney excels at the plate too. Over Team USA's six games in Tokyo,

McCleney posted nine hits. That was the most of any player in the tournament. She also walked four times, giving her an eye-popping .619 on-base percentage.

Fenton Breaks a Record

The University of Alabama won the 2012 college national championship. Jennifer Fenton was a big reason for that. The center fielder for the Crimson Tide broke University of Georgia star Nicole Barber's record in 2012 when she stole her seventy-fourth base in a row. Fenton finished her career as one of the most successful base stealers in college history, and her consecutive-steals mark remained the record through 2021. She said timing was the key to her success. "Instead of watching the ball leave the pitcher's hand, I watch the pitcher's footing," she said. "I watch the back foot lift up and start from there."

That type of performance was nothing new for the former University of Alabama standout. McCleney graduated as the Crimson Tide's all-time leader in batting average and on-base percentage. She is also second in school history in runs scored and fifth in stolen bases. It's little wonder she was named first-team All-American three times.

Running the Bases

Base running might look easy. And it is tempting to think that anyone who is a fast runner can do it. But it takes more than pure speed to be successful.

A good base runner also needs to be smart and fearless. Sometimes a pitcher has a fast

McCleney shows her excitement while crossing the plate against Team Canada at the 2020 Olympics.

release, or a catcher has a powerful arm. Stealing on them is not as likely to be easy. Good base runners know when to take off. They also must believe that they won't get thrown out.

That confidence has led to a lot of stolen bases for McCleney. Sprinting the 60 feet (18 m) to second base and beating a throw to the bag is not easy. McCleney's natural speed gives her an advantage. But she has perfected the true art of stealing.

Unlike in baseball, a softball runner cannot lead off. In softball a runner is not allowed to leave the base until the pitch leaves a pitcher's hand. That makes the first step very important. An explosive first step off the base gives the runner an advantage.

After the first step, the base runner relies on her speed to get to the next base in a hurry. McCleney's speed makes it very difficult for a catcher to throw her out.

A great first step and blazing speed are crucial. The final piece to being a successful base stealer is the slide. A good slide can allow the runner to get her foot underneath a tag and touch the base safely. A runner also can try to slide around a tag. This can be very effective, but a runner has to remember to stay in the baseline when she makes her move.

QUICK TIP:
LEARNING TO SLIDE

Sliding into the base can be a fun part of the game for base runners. It also can be one of the most enjoyable skills to learn. Charity Butler is a softball instructor in Florida. She was a star at the University of Southern Mississippi from 2003 to 2006 before playing professionally. She said the best way for a player to learn how to slide is to practice on a Slip 'n Slide water slide. "They have a blast, they overcome a lot of fears without even realizing it, and then you can translate a lot of that to the field," she said.

Another former Alabama speedster, Jennifer Fenton, combined her speed with a great feet-first sliding technique. "I think the key to her is she slides correctly, directly into the bag, and then uses a pop-up slide so that if the throw gets away, she's at third base before you can blink," Alabama coach Patrick Murphy said. "To me, that's a great technique for her. And it should teach young kids who are stealing bases to go directly into the bag and pop up."

BASES

The bases—home plate, first, second, and third— are 60 feet (18 m) apart.

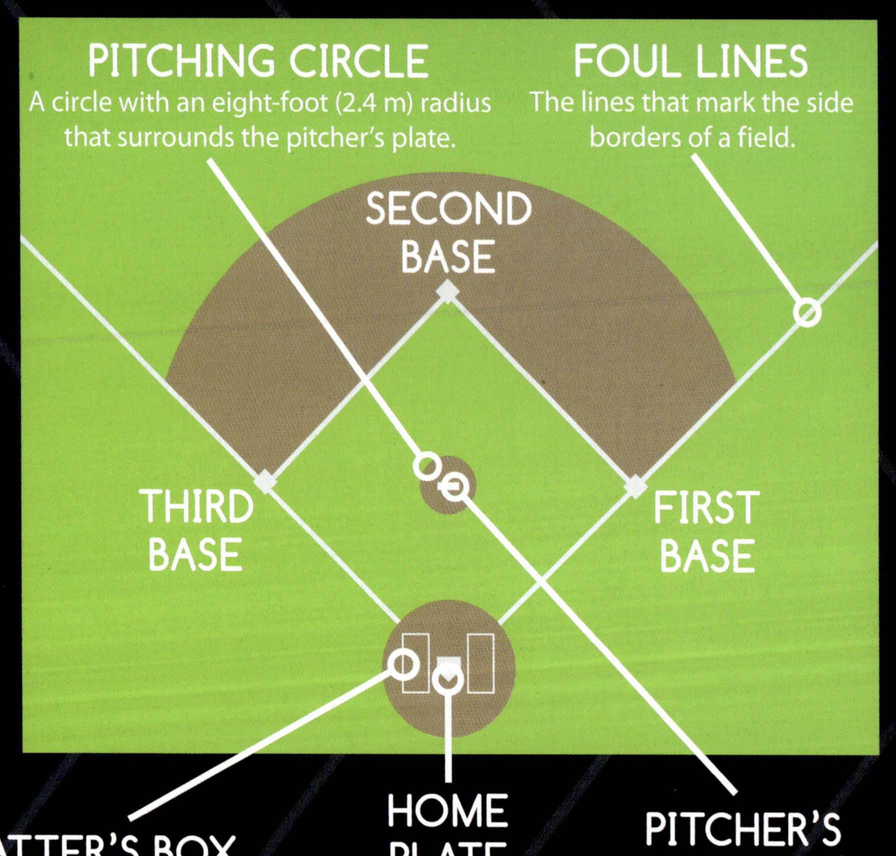

GLOSSARY

bunt
A technique used by a hitter in which she holds the bat and tries to tap the ball into play.

error
A mistake in the field made by a softball player.

fundamentals
Basic skills or building blocks of the game.

lead off
When a base runner steps off the base to get a head start to the next base before a pitch is thrown.

on-base percentage
A measure of a player's ability to reach base via a hit, walk, or being hit by pitch.

retire the side
Record the third out to end an inning.

stolen base
Running from one base to another during a pitch, not during a hit.

strike zone
The area directly over home plate and between a batter's armpits and knees. A pitch thrown here is a strike.

strikeout
An out recorded when the pitcher gets three strikes on a hitter.

umpire
An official on the field who enforces the rules of the game.

MORE INFORMATION

BOOKS

Garman, Judi, and Michelle Gromacki. *Softball Skills & Drills.*
Champaign, IL: Human Kinetics, 2011.

McDougall, Chrös. *The Olympics Encyclopedia for Kids.* Minneapolis, MN:
Abdo Publishing, 2022.

Westly, Erica. *Fastpitch: The Untold History of Softball and the Women
Who Made the Game.* New York: Touchstone, 2016.

ONLINE RESOURCES

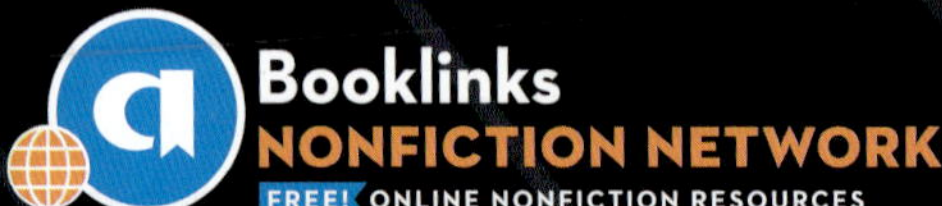

To learn more about women's softball, please visit
abdobooklinks.com or scan this QR code. These links
are routinely monitored and updated to provide the most
current information available.

PLACES TO
VISIT

National Baseball
Hall of Fame and Museum

25 Main St.
Cooperstown, NY 13326
888-425-5633
baseballhall.org

Softball has its origins in baseball. This hall of fame and museum highlights the greatest players and moments in the history of baseball.

National Softball
Hall of Fame and Museum

2801 NE 50th St.
Oklahoma City, OK 73111
405-424-5266
teamusa.org/usa-softball/usa-softball-hall-of-fame
-complex

Opened in 1957, the hall of fame is a tribute to the history of softball and many of its former star players. The museum is located at the ASA Hall of Fame Complex, which is the frequent home of the US national team and Women's College World Series.

INDEX

ABOUT THE AUTHOR

Brendan Flynn is a San Francisco resident and an author of numerous children's books.